Presidential Address

❖❖❖

A Golden Ticket Talk
by
Eric Old

to a
Meeting of the Society
at
The Coachman Hotel, Darlington
on
Saturday 21st September 1996

The Transport Ticket Society
1996

ISBN 0 903209 20 9

Published by
The Transport Ticket Society
18 Villa Road
Luton, LU2 7NT

After David Geldard, as Chairman of the Transport Ticket Society wrote to me in June 1995, notifying me that at a recent meeting, the Committee had unanimously wished for me to become President of the Society for 1995-6 - much to my surprise - and I had accepted, I was hoping that I would be able to talk enough of something of interest and relevance to the Golden Jubilee occasion, "unaccustomed as I am" etc. But that is made easier today because all of us here this afternoon are members or friends of the Transport Ticket Society, showing that "Tickets" occupy our lives to a greater or lesser degree. We decided to become members recently or a long time ago - because we have something to give to others, the opportunity of conversation or correspondence with others of similar interests, the opportunity to learn more about tickets and the likelihood of increasing the range of our own collections.

I have been asked, if possible, to talk about the origins of the Society of which I was a founder member in 1946 and which on this occasion is celebrating 50 years of existence - so I hope that I can make it interesting for all of you, whether 18 or 80 or somewhere in between!

Imagine what you would do if, as a student and collector of tickets, you thought that there seemed to be no-one else interested in them, but also knowing that there must be hundreds of varieties elsewhere to which you had no access? A very frustrating situation!

That is how it seemed to me in 1946, a year after I had been discharged from the R.A.F., (on health grounds), was back at work in a Civil service office in my home town of West Hartlepool, Co. Durham and had time to resume activity on transport subjects as a hobby. I say subjects in the plural, because I always had an interest in tickets, tramways, trolleybuses, buses and trains. I've found over the years that some people have multiple interests, whilst some are absolute specialists in apparently one subject only: there is some truth in the saying "Jack of all trades - master of none", but also in the image of absent-minded professor. I'm more of the former, although I'm sometimes "far away" when recollecting transport scenes from before the war. I cannot speak for the Methuselahs each month who know all about the railway stations of 100 years ago! Their knowledge is amazing.

With a large Society, there is room for all interests and the scope of subjects now covered in Journal - all relevant to tickets - is tremendous compared with the early years.

Tickets, tramways, trolleybuses, buses and trains I mentioned. My father didn't drive a car, so we went everywhere by public transport. The Corporation ran trams, trolleybuses and motor-buses: even before I went to compulsory school at five, in 1927, my mother wheeled me in a pushchair, (mail-cart or whatever), past the tram depot and the No.2 Gas Works, (the water-gas site of the Gas & Water Company). Numbers fascinated me. Large ones on the trams, coloured, rounded ones on the trolleybuses and buses, and numbers into thousands on tickets and EF (West Hartlepool) vehicle registrations. I was brought up in a home with a clerical background where paperwork, ledgers and rubber-stamps were

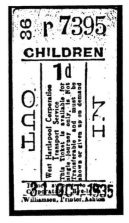

always around. My grandfather had been in charge of the local North Eastern Railway goods booking office when the Hartlepools were very busy ports. He retired in 1919 and according to the North Eastern Railway Magazine, had not been absent through illness during 52 years. He held a First Class pass enabling him to travel free on any train at any time - for 28 years of retirement!

Also, my mother did not destroy things without checking first, and this enabled me to collect tickets before 1930 and keep them past the age when so many children's items were abandoned, sold or destroyed. They also survived the years when I entered the Civil Service at Workington, Cumberland in 1938, wartime Luftwaffe bombs dropped nearby when the first Air Raid Warden in the country was killed and four and a half years in the RAF. They say that travel broadens the mind: for a ticket enthusiast, this was great opportunity to see other transport systems and collect other kinds of

tickets. In fact, this extended my interest in other places beyond West Hartlepool Corporation, of which by this time I had thousands, many collected by my parents and an Aunt and Uncle. He was the one with Yorkshire connections who talked of the "Trackless" - but mustn't digress onto that subject! "Eric, don't press your ear against that dirty pole when you are going to church", Mother used to say, as I listened for the increased humming in the wires.

My box of "other kinds" had a new fascination when combined with my Calcutta, Madras and Ceylonese tickets. I also had a very few railway tickets - which were very hard to collect

then - and some tolls which were difficult to categorize, but a shame to part with. Mainly, I equated tickets with bus and tramway issues and I discovered how many varieties existed in the towns and bus services in the North East. One could go on around journey of, say, 30 miles and come home with a colourful collection of punch-type tickets, as we did one day,

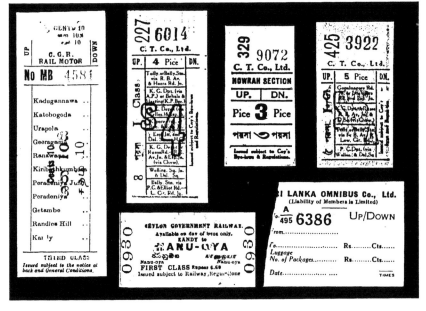

when I arranged an Omnibus Society Teeside tour, visiting the Hartlepools, Middlesbrough and Stockton, sampling routes of several operators. What a size Journal could have been then, especially if the advertisements were detailed! For example: *"Beat the paper-hanger, be a paper-saver" is being discontinued now that Hitler is dead; "Ty-Phoo Tea for indigestion" now has three separate current patterns; "Littlewoods now leaders for 27 years"*

And then a dark cloud grew: Mechanisation! All the big range of United Auto tickets and some other companies had gone over to Automatickets with stages and fares written-in; my home town was talking of experimenting with Ticket Issuing Machines, ("TIM"s). This is terrible, I thought - why not a letter to the local newspaper?

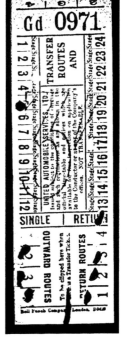

As a ticket enthusiast, it seemed a loss then, but think of the other accepted standard features of those years now gone or greatly declined - coal trains, dock shunting, steam engines everywhere, with edmondson tickets for almost all train journeys, fractions, bobs, tanners and threepenny bits, am and pm, ounces, pounds and hundredweights, inches, feet and yards, pints and gallons. An Oxo cube cost 1^d. Everyone knew that for years. If one jumped on a bus on the last part of its route, the conductor with his identifying badge, ringing two bells to the driver, would have a ticket of the minimum penny fare punched for you in no time. I think that Middlesbrough had the penny fare the longest; there was even an adult halfpenny fare in Newcastle-upon-Tyne. Well-printed tickets of different values and colours were issued then by a multitude of operators. It used to be said that more fish were in the sea than ever were caught. I feel that about the tickets which we have not seen. Conversely, there were no diesel trains, no 24-hour clock, (the war was over and civilians were back in charge), no electronics, no decimal points, no French measurements of length, height, weight or volume. The words "Land of Hope and Glory" were much more true them; people were glad to be alive - actually lucky to be alive - in the feeling of freedom after the war. There was none of the current, never-satisfied, extravagant and nanny-like "safety industry" telling us what we must do or not do.

A friend had introduced me to letter-writing, with local correspondence suggesting better bus routes in the town, and the weekly paper, *Modern Transport* published a letter of mine in August 1946, asking about preservation of historic buses when so many were still running in the North East, including Darlington trolleybus No.15. In my letter to the local paper, I claimed that the fine-printed coloured

THE NORTHERN DAILY MAIL, TUESDAY, APRIL 8, 1947.

EXPERIMENT IN BUS TICKETS

HAVING received a machine-issue type of bus ticket, with which the local Transport Department are apparently experimenting. I should like to point out some of the disadvantages to be encountered in departing from the bell-punch system because, especially where there are large numbers of passengers paying a variety of fares, the bell-punch method has proved to be the best for all concerned.

For the operator it provides the means of obtaining almost any statistics desired. For the conductor and the passenger it provides a clearly printed ticket, giving a reliable visual and audible check of each fare paid. Now, for instance, if a passenger pays twopence after nine o'clock he expects a purple ticket. If he were handed a brown one, he would immediately realize that it was one penny value and not twopence.

Mechanical systems are much more liable to break down: they issue tickets of one colour only, and have no bell to strike, thus providing much greater possibilities for misuse. No doubt passengers tried to read the faintly printed machine tickets issued recently, but they are not likely to continue doing so, and will soon just screw them up, no matter what fare has been paid.

The London Passenger Transport Board, which issues more tickets than any other undertaking, has spent years experimenting with mechanical ticket systems, but none has been found to be an improvement on the bell-punch system — the friend of the operator, the conductor, and the passenger. —A. Eric Old.

NORTHERN DAILY MAIL, THURSDAY, APRIL 10, 1947.

Printers and the Bus Tickets

[TO THE EDITOR]

A GREAT many people in West Hartlepool will be enormously interested in Mr. A. Eric Old's letter concerning a new type of bus ticket with which apparently the West Hartlepool Transport Department is experimenting.

The letter is of special interest to members of the Typographical Association whose Executive Committee in Manchester wrote its local branch as long ago as November 21, 1946, that: "The West Hartlepool transport department is experimenting with two ticket printing machines on their premises. These machines do away entirely with

the printed tram and bus ticket and are regarded by the Executive Council as a danger to the legitimate work of printers."

That is what our governing body told us. Can it be that the machines your correspondent refers to are the machines alleged to be a danger to the employers who have invested capital in bus ticket printing plant and the trade unionists who operate such plant? They could be! There is an element of doubt. When the Hartlepools Branch of the Typographical Association was apprised of the fact that a new way of dealing with bus tickets was in course of introduction in the Hartlepools they felt the need for a good deal more information on the subject.

It seemed wise, therefore, not to make any protest to the authorities until the project took definite shape and greater detail was available. Your correspondent seems to have brought us to that stage now. By April 8 employers who own bus ticket printing plant, the members of the union who operate such plant, and the travelling public are faced with what looks very much like a *fait accompli*.

No doubt the final decision will rest upon the results of the experiments in progress. In an extraordinarily lucid manner Mr. Old states the case for the retention of the present bell-punch system. Mr. Old evidently writes with close knowledge of this phase of passenger transport. He roundly declares: The bell-punch system is the friend of the Transport Committee, the conductor (does the conductors' appropriate trade union agree?) and the friend of the passenger, a formidable trio. These, of course, are not the only people the chummy bell-punch system befriends. It befriends the owners of some very highly specialized printing plant, the highly specialized workers who use it, and who, because of the division of labour, are exceedingly difficult to absorb into the main stream of the general printing industry when rendered redundant by the adoption of rivals to the system.

On all counts then— accountancy, checking receipts, advertisement revenue making, retention of valuable plant and skilled labour employed at trade union rates, and satisfaction to the travelling public —the case for the retention of the existing system is conclusive. —Arthur Bray.

tickets with the bell punch were preferable to the flimsy, poorly-printed plain specimens from machines, and that London used only pre-printed bell punch tickets. Surprisingly there was a reply from the local representative of the Typographical Association supporting me. He said that the Executive Committee of his Association regarded such, (TIM), machines as a danger to the legitimate work of printers. The machines *were* introduced on the town routes, but not for the longer Teeside services. What do printers think now, with all the instant electronic inventions, printing tickets showing enough personal information to solve a detective story?

In 1946, "Postwar" was the "in" word, and many things in everyday life were changing, with plenty of talk about how everything was going to be modernised. Being a member of the Light Railway Transport League and the Omnibus Society, I read of changes in other places and attended some outings to nearby towns where trams were being abandoned and pre-war buses replaced by new ones when supplies arrived. Some of the same friends were in both Societies and some didn't mind parting with their tickets to those who were interested in tickets. It transpired that Rae McLeod of Sunderland had a great knowledge of Sunderland tramways and the tickets of Sunderland, and one day at his home, we wondered whether there could be others as interested in tickets as we were. Rae was a tall, very thin man of about my age, then a draughtsman, I believe, and not in good health. John Farthing of Gosforth, Newcastle-upon-Tyne was very keen to find out about the Penn Bus Co., (of Buckinghamshire). He was a short, cheery banker or accountant and was soon out of breath! With me having been medically discharged from the R.A.F., we were, perhaps, an unlikely trio to launch a Society. My mother said "I don't know why you bother with tickets so much, but you do have nice friends!"

Rae suggested an insertion in a transport publication to test this possibility - and would we help? John said that he would act as Treasurer and I said that I would look after circulating and posting of tickets between members. We didn't really know what the response would be. Rae suggested the name *Ticket and Fare Collection Society.* (the words *Fare Collection* being prominent in the Bye-Law notices in Sunderland Corporation vehicles). We agreed that he would be member No.1, John Farthing, No.2, and myself as No.3. He duly published the advertisement, obtained Mr. W H Bett, the well-known author of *The Theory of Fare Collection on Railways and Tramways* as member No.4, and considered how members, (more scattered than we were), could be better informed about the Society.

When an LRTL outing to Byker, Newcastle-upon-Tyne had to be changed to Gosforth Park Races, we rode out there on an open-topped tram via the eastern route through the fields, and had special Gosforth Park tickets, which were quite rare. So, some of us collected spares, mentioning the Society. One friend, George Hearse - an early supporter of Beamish Museum and now an expert on Manx industrial archaeology, said that we were more scatty than scattered with the "Torn Ticket Society", (TTS). We didn't realise that these initials would stand for the Transport Ticket Society many years ahead! One feature which surprised me as a 24 year-old with a transport hobby, was the encouraging, professional response to newspaper letters and the willingness of operators to assist members of transport societies on visits and tours over the years, enabling so many distributions of tickets.

The response to the advertisement was good, with over twenty enquiries, if I recall correctly. Among the early applications for membership were Mr. R.J. Durrant, (No.12), Mr. J.I. Babington, (No.14), Mr. J.A. Graham, (No.21), Mr. J.C. Purton, (No.26), Mr. R. Atkinson, HM Forces, (No.27), Mr. G.H.I. Fairchild, (No.30) and Mr. J.L. King, (No.35). John Farthing dealt with the subscriptions, Rae McLeod was in consultation with Mr. G. Judd, (No.8), potential editor of the magazine or information newsletter, (They agreed to use my suggested name of *Ticketopics*), and I set about thinking how to circulate tickets. Although we used the name "Ticket and Fare Collection", we just assumed at first that it would be bus and tram tickets which everyone would want to exchange, (by contrast, the later name of the Transport Ticket Society covering road and rail equally also studies shipping, airline, tokens and some non-passenger toll and admission tickets). Look at the varied "special interests" included in the membership list nowadays! To accomplish the circulation of "spares", I thought that the best way would be to have "books" made up of 8" x 5" sheets with pouches, which would be posted from one to another,

eventually returning to "No.3 Circulation Centre". However, if the sequence was A-B-C-D-A the first time, A-D-C-B-A would be better next time, and say, A-C-D-B-A another time. There is however, a limit to such variations, even with groups E to F to G and H to J to K intermixing, and like many things, were not quite so smooth in practice. Someone, perhaps unavoidably would cause a delay, someone would expect a book or pocket to arrive and if it didn't, someone would find too many "common ones" etc. Also, the diagrammatic directioning became more tricky, but the scheme was a start, which achieved our first aspirations - to enable ticket enthusiasts to exchange their spare tickets for ones which were new to their collection.

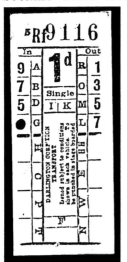

It soon became evident that some south of England members had huge collections of different London tickets, a system much more complicated than we had imagined. Also, with about half of the members being in the London area, a "London Branch" soon began. Those of us in the North east were amazed at their prolific spares, and noted how the "rarer ones" on our doorstep were appreciated.

Another surprise to us was the volume of railway ticket interest by many of the new members; some people seemed to have no difficulty in collecting them! (I found out a bit more about it in later years when we lived in Cardiff with its 21 stations and halts, and one could juggle between Queen Street and Cardiff General). So, I tried to adapt the circulating books to have either railway tickets or bus and tramway tickets.

An unexpected feature of the membership list was people writing from abroad: Mr. O. Brewer, USA, (No.33), Mr. G. Stetza, Germany, (No.35), Rev D. Ridley Chesterton, Belgian Congo, (No.42), Dr. H.A. Vreedenburg, Netherlands, (No.38), Mr. P. Boehm, Germany, (No.46) and Mr. A.F. Reinhol, (No.47). This was surprising to us, but very welcome, and still continuing of course, with some 12% of the membership having addresses beyond the United Kingdom. Personally, I had fairly frequent correspondence with Mr. Oscar Brewer of Cleveland, Ohio. I never did find out how they came to hear about the Society.

Rae McLeod did an enormous amount of work as Honorary General Secretary, building up the membership. By June 1947 there were 37 members, by August there were 43, and by July 1948, the total had reached 51. Initially the subscription was 5/-d, (25p), and 2/6d, (12½p) per year.

Ticketopics No.1 (eight pages) was printed in April 1947, beginning with an encouraging introduction by Mr. W. H. Bett, some uncertain items about railway ticket exchanges and ticket collection methods by Mr. Babington. I didn't have much to do with the contents and production of *Ticketopics*, but it appeared that Rae

OFFICIAL JOURNAL OF THE TICKET & FARE COLLECTION STY.

Vol.1. No.1 April 1947. For Private Circulation.

A LETTER FROM THE PRESIDENT.

Dear Fellow Members,

The study of Transport Tickets and fare collection methods is a large and fascinating subject, and the founders of the Ticket and Fare Collection Society are to be congratulated on their enterprise in forming an organisation to bring together those interested in it. The Society fills a real need, and I was therefore very glad to be able to place my services at its disposal when Mr. MacLeod paid me the compliment of asking me to act as President.

The launching, even in a small way, of a magazine devoted to the subject is a further valuable step in the right direction, and I feel that these pages can fulfil a really useful function, in more than one way. News of changes in ticket arrangements, articles on specialised aspects of the subject, information of permanent value for reference purposes – these can all find a useful place in this magazine. I welcome the enterprise which has made its appearance possible, and trust that it may have a long and successful career.

Yours truly,
W. H. BETT.

McLeod and Gordon Judd did not agree on some aspects of the magazine. However, it did continue up to issue No.4 in October 1947, the latter including a free gift ticket from Mr. Brewer.

The Society was still fragile and it was not helped when I had a work transfer from my home town of West Hartlepool. This was initially to London Victoria, but I managed to alter this to Llandudno, (an event which changed my life thereafter), and being in various lodgings 200 miles away, could not maintain the circulation books.

In October 1947, a Balance Sheet was produced showing that 45 members had paid £10-5s-0d, (£10.25), and ticket sales were 1/3d, (6.25p), the net carried forward was 12/8d, (63p) and the cash float in London was £1-0s-0d, so the Society was solvent in the first year. In the same month, Rae McLeod distributed a list of seventeen proposed rules to be discussed at a meeting in Newcastle-upon-Tyne. The Honorary London Branch Secretary was stated to be Mr. F. G. Williams, (No.7). He also became Circulation Book Secretary and a member of the Society Council, being so listed in the Ticket & Fare Collection Society *Journal* No.1, dated December 1st 1947. This was quick work and the 12-page Journal promised another issue six weeks later. Such co-operation by friends who could meet frequently not only saved the Society but enabled road ticket and railway ticket enthusiasts to have a better acquaintance of each other's specialities in their chosen aspect of the common interest in tickets. The London meetings at that time were held by kind permission of the Stephenson Locomotive Society at 32 Russell Road, Kensington.

No. 1.   December 1st, 1947. 3166/5

THE
TICKET & FARE-COLLECTION SOCIETY
JOURNAL.

The Ticket and Fare-Collection Society was founded in 1946 for the association of persons interested in the study of fare-collection methods and the collection of transport fare-documents. The annual subscription is 10/-

President: W. H. Bett, F.C.I.I.
Chairman: A. E. Old.

Hon. Gen. Secretary: C. R. MacLeod, 54 Otto Terrace, Sunderland.

Hon. Gen. Treasurer: J. F. Farthing, 277 Salters Road, Gosforth, Newcastle-on-Tyne, 3.

Hon. London Branch Secretary and Circulation Book Secretary: F. G. Williams, 45 Glebe Road, Finchley, London, N.3.

Hon. Exchange Pools Secretary: J. O. Guy, 40 Heckford Road, Poole, Dorset.

Hon. Information Officer: G. Judd, 40a London Road, Bromley, Kent.

Council: J. F. Farthing, C. R. MacLeod, R. A. Nash, A. E. Old, F. G. Williams.

The "Journal", the official magazine of The Ticket & Fare-Collection Society is published every six weeks. Next issue: January 15th, 1948.

In 1948, the first lady member, Miss D. Sadler joined the Society. During that year when I was in Llandudno, my activities with transport matters declined as my wife and I met, became engaged and were married within the twelve months, both being transferred to an office in Cardiff. In fact, the only 1948 T&FCS item I have is a notification from Mr. F. G. Williams announcing an Annual General Meeting, nominations for all offices and a postal ballot. This took place because Rae McLeod was *hors de combat* in the Autumn of that year.

The next item that I have is *Circular No.1*, January 1949, giving notes of monthly meetings in London. *Circular No.2*, April 1949 describes the road circulation scheme as using envelopes instead of books, containing 50 instead of 90 tickets.

TICKET & FARE-COLLECTION SOCIETY.

ANNUAL GENERAL MEETING, 1948.
This will take place on Saturday, November 20 at 32, Russell Road, Kensington (by Kensington [Olympia] Stn.) at 3 p.m. All members who can possibly attend are earnestly requested to do so.
AGENDA.
1. Minutes of A.G.M., 1947.
2. Any questions arising out of the Minutes.
3. Results of Election of Officers for 1949 (see below)
4. Any other business.
ELECTION OF OFFICERS.
This will be by means of a Postal Ballot. NOMINATIONS are requested for all offices. These are: Hon. Gen. Secretary, Hon. Gen. Treasurer, three ordinary Council members and Hon. Gen. Chairman. These nominations should be sent by November 10 at latest to F.G.WILLIAMS, 45, GLEBE ROAD, FINCHLEY, N.3, so that voting papers can be sent out in time.
[This business is being undertaken in London at the request of the Hon. Gen. Sec., Mr. MacLeod who is hors-de-combat for the moment through pressure of business.]

LONDON AREA.
The next meeting will be on Thursday, November 11 at 32, Russell Road at 7 p.m. Members will be invited to speak on subjects (of their own choice) of general interest to the Society, each speaker being limited to five minutes.

F. G. WILLIAMS
(Hon. Sec., London Area.)
OCTOBER 31, 1948

TICKET & FARE-COLLECTION SOCIETY
Circular No 2. APRIL 16, 1949.

CHANGE OF ADDRESS.
The address of the Hon. Gen. Sec. is now 40, MUSWELL ROAD, MUSWELL HILL, N.10 and you are asked to alter the Glebe Road address to this new one on any Circulation Book or Packet you receive. And would "Sammlerbrief" kindly announce this change of address!
THE MAGAZINE
Many apologies are due for the non-appearance of the Magazine, but there have been many obstacles of one sort or another. We shall make up for it before the end of the year and, in the meantime, your indulgence is requested. There are, unhappily, too few helpers and rather a lot of critics!
LONDON AREA MEETING.
This is rather short notice for the next meeting will take place next Friday (April 22) at 7 for 7.30 p.m. at 32, Russell Road, Kensington. It is proposed to let this meeting take the form of a general discussion and it will be a good opportunity for the London members to bring along what information they have gathered about the Thick Initial L.T. Bus issues recently inflicted on us.
CIRCULATION SCHEME (ROAD SERVICES).
The new system of using Envelopes instead of Books was designed so as to make the scheme simpler to handle. It is felt, too, that 50 tickets instead of 90 will help to keep down the "ballast" of 1½d 24's, 9's and 11's, etc. It was expected that there would be some criticism, but, as yet, only one person has said anything about the change and he appeared to be quite contented. There is only one drawback: the writing of the addresses on the Envelopes: this takes hours. You are warned that the first issue of the Magazine will contain a list of the names and addresses of all members and the writing of addresses on the Envelopes will be discontinued.
F. G. WILLIAMS (Hon. Gen. Sec)
40, MUSWELL ROAD, MUSWELL HILL, N.10.

By December 1949, Mr.J.C. Purton had been elected Secretary, the preliminary issue of *Newsletter* contains a paragraph about a new ticket machine introduced by London Transport on Route 1: *"....This is an invention by a Mr. Gibson..... It remains to be seen whether the machine will prove a success or not."* By October 1950, the T&FCS appeared again in the distant mail of members although the London members were said to be hale and thriving. Perhaps I missed a newsletter because this was addressed to West Hartlepool, Yorks! The subscription was reduced to 4/-d, (20p) per annum. In November 1950, *Newsletter* continued, it being noted that Mr. R. Atkinson was to act as Secretary *pro tem*; also to lower the minimum age limit for membership to fifteen. All members were asked to recruit as many as they were able and membership did grow.

TICKET AND FARE COLLECTION SOCIETY

NEWS LETTER

3107

| Preliminary Issue | December 1949 | For Members Only |

To All Members

We must apologise for the non-appearance of any magazine for the past few months, but we have been trying to find a kind friend to undertake the onerous job of duplicating the "News Letter", and at last one has come forward to offer his services. This sheet will appear monthly from now onwards.

Meetings

Good News for all London Members. The Meeting dates for the New Year have been settled, and it has been arranged to have them on the second Tuesday in each month. The dates are as follows:- Jan. 10, Feb. 14, Mar. 14, Apl. 11, May 9, Jun. 13, Jul. 11, Aug. 8, Sep. 12, Oct. 10, Nov. 14, Dec. 12. The address of the Meeting Place:- 32 Russell Road, Kensington W.14.

News Items

It would be greatly appreciated if all Members, London and Provincial, would communicate all items of news of interest to ticket collectors, such as new issues, new operators, operators swapping over to ticket machines, new routes, fare stage changes, and anything of interest to transport enthusiasts to :- A.W. McCall, 7 Maple Grove, London, N.W.9., for inclusion in this "News Letter".

London Transport's New Ticket Machines

A new ticket machine was introduced by London Transport on buses operating on Route 1 (Willesden and Lewisham) from Cricklewood Garage. The machine, which is the invention of a Mr. Gibson, former manager of the London Transport Punch shops at Stockwell, appears to be a combination of the best ideas of the "T.I.M." and "Setright" machines, and issues a ticket of the size of the "T.I.M.", but printed vertically instead of horizontally. It indicates fare paid, stage boarded (as a numeral), route number on which issued, date of issue, class (Ordy., Child, Midday, Return &c.), serial number and machine number. It remains to be seen whether the machine will prove a success or not.

Secretary

Our former Secretary, Mr. F.G. Williams, has had to resign owing to pressure of private business, and Mr. J.C. Purton, of 109 Priory Park Road, London N.W.6., has been elected Secretary of the Society, and any communications concerning the Society should be sent to him. Communications concerning this "News Letter" should be sent to the Editor, Mr. A.W. McCall, 7 Maple Grove, Kingsbury, London N.W.9.

Workman Return Tickets...L.T.E. Trans & Trolleybuses

The 5d. Workman Return Tickets of the L.T.E. Trans and Trolleybuses are now appearing overprinted with a large "R" instead of a diagonal line. It has not yet appeared on other values, but it is extremely possible that it may do so at a later date.

Eastern National Change-Over.

It has been noticed that Conductors on Route 10 (Bow and Chelmsford) have mostly all been equipped with the "Setright Speed" machine in place of the very cumbersome "Willibrew" machines.

Greenline Tickets

The thick initial letter which has been in use for some time on Central Buses has now been extended to Greenline Coach tickets, including the 6-day weekly tickets. The panels on the reverse side have now been altered, and simply show excess fares to and from London, the Child panel not being necessary, as Child tickets, like adult tickets, are punched at Stage Boarded.

his is an appropriate time for me to come to a conclusion. *Newsletter* continued for 2,500 pages up to the end of 1963, then becoming the *Journal of the Transport Ticket Society*, which reached 15,000 pages by the end of the last year, 1995. I mentioned that my parents were very good in not disturbing tickets which I collected and I must say that my wife is also very careful with all the transport items which I have built up over the years.

My friends John Farthing died in 1952 and Rae McLeod in 1970, so I am the only original T&FCS member still around. I am glad that we have been able to keep these Society notes for 50 years and hope that you find my recollections interesting. May I quote an extract from a letter of mine printed in the February 1991 *Journal*? "If it hadn't been for the London Branch, I don't think the Society would have survived"; it enabled meetings to take place with a nucleus of enthusiasts who had much greater knowledge of tickets than we had in Co.Durham and the meetings led to the regular monthly *Newsletter* which drew in more members and ticket news of all kinds.

I am sure that everyone, whether pre-war collector or the newest member has tales to tell about how he started and is building up his collection and his knowledge of tickets. And are there not any lady ticket students, business people and collectors who would like to join? Perhaps enthusiasts in the year 2046 putting their identity cards into their automated transport with their fares debited instantly from their bank accounts will also say of us today: "They had fine tickets in those days".

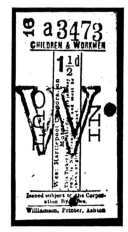

Let us hope that the Society will continue to flourish for another 50 years! So keep in touch, keep collecting - it's good to talk, especially ticket-talk!

Eric Old
September 1996